AF662681

Mastering Salary Negotiations

How to skilfully negotiate the best remuneration package

Jayant Neogy

UNICORN BOOKS Pvt. Ltd.

Distributors

PUSTAK MAHAL

Publishers
UNICORN BOOKS, New Delhi-110002
E-mail: unicornbooks@vsnl.com
Website: www.unicornbooks.in • www.kidscorner.in

Distributors
Pustak Mahal, Delhi
J-3/16 , Daryaganj, New Delhi-110002
☎ 23276539, 23272783, 23272784 • *Fax:* 011-23260518
E-mail: info@pustakmahal.com
Website: www.pustakmahal.com

London Office
5, Roddell Court, Bath Road, Slough SL3 OQJ, England
E-mail: pustakmahaluk@pustakmahal.com

Sales Centre
10-B, Netaji Subhash Marg, Daryaganj, New Delhi-110002
☎ 23268292, 23268293, 23279900 • *Fax:* 011-23280567
E-mail: rapidexdelhi@indiatimes.com

Branch Offices
Bangalore: ☎ 22234025
E-mail: pmblr@sancharnet.in • pustak@sancharnet.in
Mumbai: ☎ 22010941
E-mail: rapidex@bom5.vsnl.net.in
Patna: ☎ 3294193 • *Telefax:* 0612-2302719
E-mail: rapidexptn@rediffmail.com
Hyderabad: *Telefax:* 040-24737290
E-mail: pustakmahalhyd@yahoo.co.in

© Copyright : Unicorn Books

ISBN 978-81-7806-055-2

Edition : 2007

The Copyright © of this book as well as all matter contained herein (including illustrations) rests with UNICORN BOOKS. No person shall copy the name of the book, its title design, matter and illustrations in any form and in any language, totally or partially or in any distorted form. Anybody doing so shall face legal action and will be responsible for damages.

Printed at : Param Offsetters, Okhla, New Delhi-110020

Contents

1 Introduction

In this chapter:

- Acknowledgement
- Preface
- What this book contains
- Conventions used in this book

Acknowledgement

The overwhelming response to my earlier two books, *Winning Resume* and *Sure Success in Interviews* encourages and sustains me. It is good to know that, in some small measure, these books have been of use to so many readers in their quest for a better job. Emboldened by their response, I have written this book, the third of the series. It is a logical step for a job-seeker after he or she has written a good résumé, been successful in interviews and has finally secured a job offer.

Now that you have done so well and come so far, use this book to get the very best in the salary and compensation package for yourself.

This book would not have been possible without steady support and continuing encouragement from my publishers and my understanding wife. I thank them all sincerely. Above all, I thank you, my readers, without whom none of my books would have ever been written!

—Jayant Neogy
Palam Vihar, Gurgaon

Preface

There was a time when salaries were virtually non-negotiable. All government jobs had fixed salary grades. Depending on your qualifications and experience, you would be assigned a salary, determined by the organisation's official salary structure and not by your actual market value. Most of the private firms also followed a similar policy for determining salaries. Therefore, securing the job was all that mattered. The salary automatically followed.

Not any more! All of you are aware how business process outsourcing (BPO) has opened up the Indian job market to multinational companies, who have transferred many of their back office and front office operations to India. Indian companies are also modifying their hiring and compensation strategies to remain competitive. The key word here is *competition*. Because of fierce competition, organisations want to negotiate salaries to cut down payroll costs. On the other hand, alternative job opportunities allow employees to negotiate their true market value. As a result, salaries and compensation packages have become negotiable as never before.

Negotiation is no longer a dirty word when it comes to agreeing on what you should be paid for the job. Beware, however, that you do not try to drive so hard a bargain that you frighten off potential employers. While you want a good salary, you must ensure that the employers also feel they have gained a valuable employee. In short, you must learn to negotiate in a "win-win" situation. Both parties must feel good when it is over!

The need for win-win skills has really become very important after globalisation and outsourcing became a reality of business life. In this environment, innovative and sharp-witted salary negotiation skills have become as critical for your career growth as penning a winning résumé or learning how to ace that interview.

My earlier books in this series, *Winning Résumés* and *Sure Success in Interviews* were both received well by the readers. Some of them wrote to say that the books have really helped them in the job market. Their positive feedback encourages me to write this book and thus complete a set of three books. Together they will help any job aspirant, new or a veteran, to put his or her career quest on steroids!

To the readers of my earlier books, sincere thanks for your support and best wishes to all of you seeking to enhance your careers!

—JL Neogy

What this Book Contains

The six chapters and the Annexure of this book contain all that you need to know to negotiate salary packages. We cover strategies for salary reviews, preparation for performance appraisals and techniques tailored specially for fresh graduates. Quizzes are included after chapters 5 and 6, along with answers in the Annexure. They will help you to find out how well you have absorbed the principles, advice and tips given in this book.

This book will take you through preparation, information gathering, and evaluation of offers and negotiation of the compensation package right to the closing of negotiations. For fresh entrants to the job-seeking fraternity, we have specially included the last chapter, which covers tips on negotiations, appraisals and salary review.

We recommend that you read the book in the sequence it is written, pausing for the tests. It will give you a comprehensive and in-depth understanding of the art and craft of salary negotiations as a whole. For fresh job seekers, we recommend that you read chapter 6 in detail. Otherwise, you can begin with any topic that interests you since each chapter is self-contained.

We give a brief outline of the chapters below, along with our suggestions on who should begin where:

Chapter 1 is what you are reading at present. Start here to get a feel of the contents and of the design of the book, including the conventions we have used to make the book easy to read and quick to refer to.

Chapter 2 is about preparations. If you wish to get an insight into the information you need for negotiations and tips on where to get it, begin here.

Chapter 3 is about evaluating a job offer and its compensation package. We show you how to research the organisation and the job. Begin here if you already have an offer in hand. If you are lucky enough to have more than one, this chapter will tell you how to compare them objectively.

Chapter 4 is the heart of this book. We cover negotiations in depth and in detail. Read this chapter to understand strategies. Learn how to handle a premature request for your salary expectation and to respond constructively to it. For tips on responding to unsatisfactory offers and for ideas on negotiating the benefits package, start here.

Chapter 5 is on closing the deal. Start here to master the skill to close a negotiation, commit to the new employer and separate gracefully from the current one.

Chapter 6 is for fresh job aspirants and for those preparing for performance evaluation and salary review. Begin here if you are a fresh graduate or if you are to be evaluated in your current job.

NOTE In addition, there are two quizzes, one each at the end of chapters 4 and 5. We suggest that you do not attempt the quizzes before reading the relevant chapters. For correct answers, see the Annexure at the end of this book.

Conventions Used in this Book

This book is designed for easy reading and quick reference. We have used attractive graphics to direct your attention to the top answers, tips, pitfalls and explanatory notes using little icons that you see below.

TOP 	A part of any negotiation will involve answering difficult questions. You have to give a well thought out reply to avoid a trap. Our suggested answers are designed to do just that. These answers are marked with a "TOP" sign and the icon of an upraised thumb.
TIP 	When important information exceeds a few lines and extends over an entire paragraph, a wise owl identifies the "TIP". You will find these tips distributed throughout this book, guiding you from one important tip to the next. Follow the owl and rapidly assimilate many good ideas.
TRAP 	All endeavours have dangers and pitfalls. Negotiating your salary is no exception. It is easy to overlook something important or to give out a wrong signal, jeopardising your chances. Caution is called for. A "TRAP" is clearly identified in this book by the familiar skull and crossbones. Beware when you see this symbol and heed the warning to save yourself grief!
NOTE 	Additional information or explanatory notes are identified by a pen and ink symbol. Read the "NOTE" for more information on an important topic.

2 Preparation

In this chapter:

- We help you to find out if you are really ready to start negotiations.
- How to make sure that you have the information you need about the organisation and the job.
- Tips on how to know your market value.
- We show you techniques for developing your personal strategy for negotiations.

Are You Prepared?

If you are like me, then before you start off on a journey you will probably go through a mental checklist. Do you have the ticket? What about money? Do you know your destination address? You will mentally tick off these and many other questions about the little things required to make your journey successful.

In the same way, let us go through a checklist to make sure that you have not left out any major step before negotiations begin. The stakes are high. Whether you get a good deal or not will depend on the quality and thoroughness of your preparation.

A Checklist for You

Your negotiation strategy will depend upon several factors. Among them:

- Your market value
- The employer
- Your own negotiating style
- Current market demand for your skills
- Quality and extent of the competition

In this book, we help you to evolve and master your very own negotiating strategy after taking all these factors into account.

When Can You Begin Negotiations?

Remember that you are not in a position to negotiate money (and/or any other benefits) until after the "sale" is made. In this case, your job application and the subsequent interviews are all part of your sales effort or "sales pitch". You are trying to convince the interviewer that you are the best candidate for the job. The sale is completed only when you have the job offer in hand.

NOTE The offer itself may range from a verbal "We are ready to make an offer" to a formal letter which has all the details in writing. Regardless of the exact nature of the offer, it is important to realise that without an offer, you cannot begin negotiations. Until that point in time, you cannot negotiate the "what" of the offer, you can only negotiate the "if" and the "when".

TRAP Do not begin negotiations by telling the employer what your salary expectations are. This advice may sound trivial, but it is vital for success of the negotiations. Before the formal offer, the employer will try to gauge your expected salary so that he or she can start low and bargain even lower.

TOP Here is your best strategy. Meet every attempt that the employer makes to bring up salary issues by something similar to "I am ready to consider your very best offer". Do not indicate a salary or compensation package at this stage, even though you do have a clear target figure in mind.

TIP If you follow this strategy, you will get the best possible initial offer from the employer. We call it "initial" because it is exactly that. Very few employers will make a first offer that is "carved in stone". Even if the employer says that their salary structure is rigid, you will be able to negotiate some benefits and advantages later if you have not already committed yourself.

Do You Have the Right Information?

Information you need for salary negotiations is in equal measures about the employer and about yourself. You must know the employer's salary range for the job you have applied for. You will also need to know their policy about salary reviews and increments. You require a "feel" for their negotiation strategy. Do they bargain hard or do they have fixed scales into which they will find you a slot? The company's annual report will give you some answers.

Information about the company's style of negotiation, however, will be harder to get. You may have to find and talk to current or former employees. Your negotiation strategy will be only as strong as your depth of knowledge about the potential employer. So, collect as much information about it as possible.

NOTE It is equally important to have a realistic knowledge of your market value for the job. While you may have a good idea about your intrinsic value, which depends on your qualification, experience and track record, your market value will change according to the laws of supply and demand. Thus, your area of specialisation may see a boom, boosting your market value, or your industry may be in a slump and you may find that job offers are very hard to get, or that the pay is very poor.

Build your negotiating strategy to suit your personal negotiating style. Are you aggressive and extroverted or do you prefer a quiet presentation based on facts and figures? Do you relish a face-to-face combat with the employer or do you prefer to reply to an offer in writing, after careful thought?

TIP It is important to find what you are good at and negotiate using your strength. Later in this chapter, we will help you to determine your own strengths and weaknesses. This knowledge will help you to develop your own strategy, one that you are comfortable with.

Negotiation Preliminaries

Examine the offer you have received to locate incomplete information that needs further clarification. You are also trying to find out opportunities for further negotiations.

Raise a Few Questions

Seek clarifications for any incomplete information. In addition, obtain information such as:

- "What are the promotional opportunities of this position?"
- "How frequently will my performance be reviewed?"
- "What is the expected salary progression in the first three to five years for a good performer?"

NOTE In particular, note if answers are freely given along with assurances like "we reward good performance", or "for a good performer, there is nothing to worry regarding career progress". While these assurances are not strictly part of the written offer, they will stand you in good stead in future negotiations. You will also get a feel for the employer's negotiating style.

Who Should You Speak to?

If the offer is not acceptable to you in its present form you may reject it, or make a counteroffer of your own. Before you do so, find out who is the final hiring authority. It is usually your would-be boss, but not always. Hiring authorisation may actually come from a level above him or her. There will also be input from the human resource development (HRD) or personnel department. The key is to know *who* makes the final decisions.

TIP Your negotiation strategy will require you to reach the person with the final power to alter the terms of the offer. You will need to convince him or her to accept your counteroffer. Before doing so, however, thoroughly check the offer you have received. Use a checklist like the sample given here to do so.

Job Offer Checklist

Have this job offer checklist ready with you when you evaluate the offer. If you do not use a checklist, you may miss important details. The checklist is vital for comparing two offers if you are lucky enough to have more than one in hand.

What is given below is a rather comprehensive list; therefore, every item will not necessarily apply to you or to a specific offer.

1. **Job Details**

   Look for Title, Reporting to, Starting Date.

2. **Salary Details**

   Check Base Salary, Incentive and Profit-sharing Bonus, Commission, Signing-on Bonus, Stock Options, Pension, Provident Fund.

3. **Insurance**

   Check Medical Insurance, Life Insurance, Accidental Death, Disability Benefits, Travel Insurance, Dependant Insurance.

4. **Leave**

   Determine Earned Leave, Casual Leave, Medical Leave, Paid Holidays, Overtime, Compensatory Offs.

5. **Other Benefits**

   There may also be Club Membership, Car and Driver, Travelling Allowance, Reimbursement of Tuition Fees, Training Sponsorship, Relocation Allowance etc.

   Using this guideline, prepare a checklist of your own.

Gathering Information

It is not very surprising that all of us have some difficulty in seeing ourselves exactly as others see us. Few of us want to accept our own shortcomings. Some of us see our own selves much larger and more important than we really are. Others amongst us, due to lack of self-confidence, see ourselves smaller than our true worth.

NOTE As you can easily see, wrong impressions of our own selves will lead to poor negotiation success. If you overstate your worth, the employer may consider you boastful, untrustworthy and unsuitable for the job. On the other hand, if you sell yourself short, you will not get the salary and compensation you deserve.

To negotiate well, therefore, you require information about your employer, the business or industry segment to which the job belongs and, above all, about your true market value and your preferred negotiation style. In this section, we walk you through each of these information segments.

Your Employer and Their Business

The most convenient source of information about a business organisation is the balance sheet of the company, included in its annual report to the shareholders. You will get information about the organisation's size, growth plans, track records and even information on its salary structure. The organisation's past performance, its track record, will tell you much about the future growth avenues for its employees. You will see whether the organisation is growing or remaining static, or is in decline. The chairman's report will speak of the growth in sales and profits, of the addition of new products or facilities and the organisation's market share.

NOTE If you can gain access to the records of the local chamber of commerce, there will be reports containing similar information as to what you can collect from the annual reports. Usually, chamber of commerce information is not open to the public. However, if you know some other member organisation, you can get the information you need.

Business weekly and monthly magazines carry special reports on many important organisations. Magazines dealing with the stock market, such as *Dalal Street Journal* and many others, have similar information. These reports not only tell you many valuable things about your potential employer, but also have information on the industry segment to which the employer's business belongs. Future growth opportunities may depend very much on the upsurge or downturn of the relevant business segment.

TIP

In general, look for a market leader or one with fast growth record in a business segment that is doing well and sees strong future growth potential. For example, at the time of writing this book, businesses dealing with Information Technology, Business Process Outsourcing and Biotechnology appear to have strong, sustained growth prospects. On the other hand, the Jute industry appears to be languishing.

Here are some possible sources for information about organisations, businesses and specific companies:

- Personal contacts.
- Your institute's career planning and placement offices.
- Classified advertisements in national and local newspapers.
- Professional associations and their journals.
- Trade magazines.
- Internet networks and resources.
- Government employment exchange offices.
- Private employment agencies and career consultants.

Your Market Value

You know what your qualifications and experiences are. If they happen to be in the business areas that are doing well, you too will enjoy a high market value. Qualification and experience in computer sciences, a good MBA degree or a degree from a well-known engineering institute enhances your desirability to the prospective employer and your market value rises.

NOTE Sources such as annual reports and wage surveys published in business magazines will tell you much about the going wages in different businesses and industries. You can find, for instance, what a computer engineer with three years' experience or a fresh MBA should expect. Regular study of this kind of information will help you to build up, and update, a market value profile for yourself. Such information is invaluable for setting realistic yet attractive salary goals for your own self.

Strengths and Weaknesses

In addition to market value, it is important to know your own strengths and weaknesses. SWOT analysis is a very useful technique that many use to know themselves. The acronym, SWOT, is made up of four factors: Strengths, Weaknesses, Opportunities and Threats. Major business houses and industrial organisations undertake SWOT analysis before formulating their long-term business plans. It is indeed a powerful tool. As an individual, you too can apply its principles to identify your personal strengths and weaknesses.

TIP Consider doing a full SWOT analysis if you are planning your career in detail. For salary negotiations, however, analysis of your Strengths and Weaknesses is enough.

Self-analysis

Write down a list of your strengths. Apart from academic qualifications, look for strength factors such as leadership qualities, ability to solve problems, interpersonal skills, ability to perform well under pressure and the ability to produce high quality work well within deadlines. In each case, recall actual examples from your past experience demonstrating that you do have these qualities.

TOP If you are a fresh graduate, look for examples from your academic life and from your extra-curricular activities. As you recall and jot down instances that have actually happened, you will be surprised how many positive things you can unearth about yourself.

A list of your strengths will help you to emphasise your suitability for the job over other candidates. Throughout the interviews and during the salary negotiations, use your strengths to reinforce your worth to the employer.

Prepare a small outline and keep it handy during your interviews and during the salary negotiation process. There will be occasions when you will be able to quote from these notes to underline your value to the potential employer. When the employer is thinking of the cost of hiring you, it is your responsibility to remind him or her of the value you will bring in exchange for that cost.

TOP Now write down your weaknesses. You should be both dispassionate and objective when you do so. A clear knowledge of your weaknesses will help you plan your answers. For example, if academic qualifications are not your strong point, focus on your work experience and achievements on the job. On the other hand, if you are short on experience, highlight your academic qualifications and extra-curricular accomplishments.

Concentrate on traits of your character. For instance, if you are impatient, or given to impulses, avoid accepting any offer on the spot. Ask for time to think the offer over, get the offer in writing whenever possible and then take your time before responding.

NOTE A thorough understanding of how your mind works will help you to plan a negotiation strategy that will work well for you. You can compensate for either boastfulness or timidity if you know how you usually respond. Seek inputs from your family members, friends or colleagues so that you are aware of how you appear to others.

You need not go through a psychiatric evaluation or a personality change. All that you need is to be made aware of those traits that may work against you. Often, just being aware and on your guard is quite enough.

S&W Analysis Form

Here is a model Strength and Weakness analysis form. Modify and edit the form to suit your own case.

Rate your strengths and weaknesses on a scale of 1 to 4. The rating scale is 1 = Poor, 2 = Fair, 3 = Good, 4 = Excellent.

Strength Chart

Factor	Rating
Professional degree or diploma	
Class obtained by you	
Rating of your institute	
Work experience	
Rating of your past employer	
Your level of responsibility	
Affiliation to professional organisations	
How well is the organisation known?	
Managerial skills (*)	
Problem-solving skills (*)	
Leadership skills (*)	

(*) **Note:** *If you rate these high, you should be ready with actual examples that demonstrate the abilities you claim.*

Highlight all the strengths in which you score 3 or 4. Strengths in which you score 1 or 2 are best left out of any interview or salary negotiation discussions. Proper use of your strengths is one of the most effective negotiating strategies that you can have.

Weakness Chart

Use a scale of 1 to 2. 1 should stand for a minor weakness and 2 for a significant one.

Weakness	Severity
Gap in employment history/frequent job changes	
Instance of being asked to leave a job	
Disciplinary action of any kind	

TRAP You must be very careful in dealing with weaknesses. It is a very bad idea to lie. As a first step, do not volunteer information about any of your weaknesses. If you are asked questions on gaps in employment history or frequent job changes see if you have a good (but true) reason such as ill health, financial constraints or being forced to leave your job to look after your family. The most difficult questions refer to job loss, redundancy or disciplinary action.

Since the employer will almost certainly carry out a background check before hiring you, it is really the best policy to be truthful, regardless of its impact on your job prospects.

In summary, our advice is to know your weaknesses, even the rather damaging ones, since the knowledge will help you formulate your best negotiating strategy and keep your salary expectations realistic.

A Mind Game

So far, we have concentrated on information: information about the employer, your market value, your strengths and weaknesses. We now go beyond facts to mental preparation. Like cricket, negotiation too is a mind game. You must be in the right frame of mind. To the employer, you should appear confident and yet not cocky, informed and yet not pedantic, eager and yet not desperate so that you create just the right impression.

Here are some guidelines to bring out the best in you as you negotiate.

Believe That Everything is Negotiable

Everything is negotiable! Every new job and every performance review is an opportunity to negotiate basic salary, various kinds of bonuses, benefits, stock options, and other incentives that add to your job satisfaction and provide you with financial security.

NOTE The salary package is worth negotiating because it is more than money. The value of the package is a measure of your worth. Therefore, getting what you deserve is both financially rewarding and good for your morale at the same time. If you believe in your self-worth, you will believe in negotiating to get recognition that is due to you.

Learn the Power Factors

To strengthen your morale and confidence in your own negotiating skills, understand what factors are important in any salary negotiation. Some of the factors will work in your favour and others will favour the employer. You can develop and fine-tune your negotiation strategy if you understand how these factors influence negotiations.

Pay particular attention to the following:

Business Climate Factors

These factors include the overall state of India's economy and of the industry you wish to join. You should know the current employment picture and the present demand for people with your skills.

Profitability Factors

These include the businesses and the organisation's position in the business cycle. Ask yourself questions like:

- Is it a new industry with good growth prospects?
- Is the industry stable with steady but slow growth?
- Is the industry in decline and will jobs shrink in the next few years?

The employer's ability to pay and your rate of growth will depend on these factors. You can easily appreciate the difference between pay and promotion prospects between say, information technology (IT) and the coal industry today!

Employer's Factors

Try to find out how urgent it is for the company to fill the vacancy. For instance, it is far more urgent to fill a vacancy for a new project than to fill a trainee position in a large organisation. If you are just one of very many similarly qualified and experienced candidates, you will have little room to negotiate. However, if you are one of the few possessing a special skill that the organisation needs urgently, you are in a far better position to negotiate.

Applicant's Factors

If you have other job offers in hand, you can be choosier. If you already have a good job, you can negotiate much better than if you are trying to enter the job market for the first time.

Understanding these power factors will help you to shape your own successful negotiating strategy. It will tell you, realistically, how far you can go and what you can expect. It will lift your negotiating skills from a hit-or-miss affair to a planned strategy.

Negotiate for a Win-Win

Developing a win-win attitude is the most important part of your mindset. Negotiations are often played out as a win-lose game, just like a one-day game of cricket. If one side wins, the other must lose. This is not so in a salary negotiation scenario.

NOTE Remember that it is a two-way process. You and your prospective employer are each trying to get something you need. You need the job and a good salary package. The employer needs a good employee. Therefore, a well-conducted negotiation will end in both sides gaining what they want. Both sides win!

So how exactly do you undertake a win-win negotiation? We will devote the rest of this chapter to discuss that with you. Here is the basic approach.

Define Your Dream Job

Begin by defining your dream job to yourself. It is that combination of money and job description that, taken together, make up all that you hope to get from the job. You can define what is an attractive compensation package considering your market value and the status of your prospective employer. You can outline what your job title, responsibilities and career growth opportunities should be. Write it all down and use this document to evaluate job offers. The comparison will help you to separate the unacceptable from the negotiable offers.

Employer's Dream Offer

You can be sure that the organisation has a dream offer too. Amongst other things, there will be a target salary and compensation package based on the organisation's own wage policy and industrial or business practice applicable to them.

NOTE Employers will usually like to pay 90% of the mid-point of the salary grade applicable to the position advertised, or less if possible. They will also like to include a non-disclosure (or secrecy) agreement and would like you to join tomorrow!

Keep these facts in mind while negotiating. It will help you decide when to bargain hard and when to make a compromise.

Your Attitude During Negotiations

When you receive the offer, your status changes. Before you got the offer, you were the supplicant and the employer was the giver of gifts. Now, the atmosphere becomes more like a transaction between equals. Therefore, the way you carry yourself must also change to reflect the changed situation.

TOP Firstly, do not give away your feelings when an offer is made. Remain cool and appear detached. Negotiate as if you have nothing to lose. Secondly, reveal as little as possible in response to verbal offers. Say nothing if the spoken figures appear generous. Similarly, say nothing even if you do not like what you hear. Remember that the longer you can hold out for what you want, the more likely you are to get it. Use silence as a powerful bargaining tool. Let the silence linger. If the employer presses you for a response, silence can be a very effective way to deal with such pressure.

Do Not be the First to Mention Money

Think of the following situations and how they affect the outcome of the negotiations:

- If you mention a figure first and you are too low, they win.
- If you mention a figure first and you are too high, you may be eliminated and you lose.
- If you mention a figure first and you happen to be just right, you lose the possibility of getting more. You lose again.

In all these cases, you lose!

Accept Gracefully

Follow these tips and, eventually, a time will come when you realise that you have negotiated your way to a very good job offer. Or, the best offer on the table is simply not good enough for you and you would rather wait for an offer from another organisation.

NOTE In either case, respond with grace. It is now time to drop your flat and unemotional negotiating attitude. If you have negotiated well, the offer you have accepted should make you happy. It is now time to show your happiness and make your employer feel good as well. Even if you cannot accept their best offer, do so without malice. You never know, you may be negotiating with them again some day!

3 Evaluation

In this chapter:

- We tell you how and where to look for the information you need to evaluate job offers..
- We explain techniques for evaluation of job content and the benefits package.
- The Balance Sheet approach for evaluating and comparing offers is explained.

A First Look at a Job Offer

When you receive a job offer, it is unlikely that you will either accept on the spot, or reject it out of hand. Instead, you will study the offer and see if you can negotiate improvements. You will also compare it with other offers that you may have. In addition to the offer, you will also evaluate the organisation.

To do all this, you need time. Fortunately, most organisations will not expect you to accept or reject their offer immediately.

For a preliminary assessment, look at the organisation and the job being offered to you. Will the organisation be a good place to work? Will the job be interesting? Are there opportunities for advancement? Is the salary fair? Does the employer offer good benefits? If you have not worked out exactly what you want, here is a guide for a preliminary assessment.

The Organisation

Let us tackle the organisation. Factors to consider include the organisation's business or activity, financial condition, age, size, and location where you will work.

Where to Look?

You can get background information about an organisation, particularly a large one, on its Website. You can also take a direct approach and telephone its public relations office. A public company's annual report speaks about its corporate philosophy, history, products or services, goals, and financial status.

Many large organisations advertise by publishing reports describing their programmes and missions. Press releases, company newsletters or magazines, and recruitment brochures can also be useful. Ask the organisation for any item that might interest a prospective employee. If possible, speak to current or former employees of the organisation.

Background information on the organisation may be available at your public or college library. If you cannot get an annual report, check the library for reference directories that may provide basic facts about the company, such as earnings, products and services, and number of employees.

TIP

Reports about an organisation in financial magazines and newspapers can tell a great deal about its successes, failures, and plans for the future. You can identify articles on a company by looking under its name in periodicals or business magazines. Generally, the past two to three years' records are all that you need.

What to Look For?

Having collected as much information as possible about your target organisation, try to answer the following questions:

1. *Does the organisation's business or activity match your own interests and work ethics?*

It is easier to apply yourself to the work if you are enthusiastic about what the organisation does.

2. *How will the size of the organisation affect you?*

NOTE

Large firms generally offer a greater variety of training programmes and career paths, more managerial levels for advancement, and better employee benefits than small firms. Large employers may also have more advanced technologies. However, jobs in large firms tend to be highly specialised and learning opportunities could be limited.

On the other hand, jobs in small firms often offer broader authority and responsibility, a closer working relationship with top management, and a chance to clearly see your contribution towards success of the organisation.

3. *Should you work for a relatively new organisation or one that is well established?*

New businesses have a high failure rate, but for many people, the excitement of helping create a company and the potential for sharing in its success more than offset the risk of job loss. However, it may be just as exciting and rewarding to work for an established firm that is expanding and innovating rapidly.

4. *Does it make a difference to you if the company is private or public?*

An individual or a family usually controls a privately owned company where key jobs are reserved for only relatives and friends. A board of directors responsible to the stockholders controls a publicly owned company and key jobs are usually open to anyone. However, large public sector organisations tend to work by the rulebook that does not reward enterprise or initiative.

5. *Is the organisation in a business or industry segment with favourable long-term prospects?*

The most successful firms tend to be in industries that are growing rapidly.

The Job

Let us now look closely at the job itself. Even if everything else about the job is attractive, you will be unhappy if you dislike the day-to-day part of the work. It is difficult to determine all the aspects of the job in advance, but if you have discussed your job content and your duties and responsibilities during interviews, you should have a fairly good idea. Take the following factors into account while evaluating the job:

1. *Where is the job located?*

If the job is in another region of the country, you need to consider the cost of living, the availability of housing and transportation, and the quality of educational and recreational facilities in that part of the country. Even if the job location is in your area, you should consider the time and expense of travelling to and from work.

2. *Does the work match your interests and make good use of your skills?*

The duties and responsibilities of the job should be explained in enough detail to answer this question.

3. *How important is the job in this company?*

An explanation of where you fit in the organisation and how you are supposed to contribute to its overall objectives should give you an idea of the job's importance.

4. *Are you comfortable with the hours?*

NOTE Most jobs involve regular hours such as 44 to 48 hours a week, during the day, Monday through Friday, with perhaps a half-day on Saturdays. Other jobs require night, weekend, or holiday work. In addition, some jobs routinely require overtime to meet deadlines or sales or production goals, or to better serve customers. Consider the effect the work hours will have on your personal life.

5. *How long do most people who enter this job stay with the company?*

High turnover can mean dissatisfaction with the nature of the work or something else being not quite right about the job.

6. *Opportunities offered by employers.*

A good job offers you opportunities to learn new skills, increase your earnings, and rise to positions of greater authority, responsibility, and prestige. Lack of opportunities can dampen interest in the work and result in frustration and boredom.

The company should have a training plan for you. What valuable new skills does the company plan to teach you?

NOTE The employer should give you some idea of promotion possibilities within the organisation. What is the next step on the career ladder? If you have to wait for a job to become vacant before you can be promoted, how long does this usually take? When opportunities for advancement do arise, will you compete with applicants from outside the company? Can you apply for jobs for which you qualify elsewhere within the organisation, or is mobility within the firm limited?

Congratulations! You have now reviewed the company and the preliminaries of the job offer. If the offer meets with your target so far, it is time to examine the job content and the compensation package in detail.

Evaluating Alternative Offers

It is now time to closely examine the job content as well as the salary and benefits. We will do so to compare the job offer with the target we have drawn up as well as with any other job offers that you may have in hand.

We break up the offer into two major parts. One part deals with the job content. It contains things like your job title, your reporting level, your duties and responsibilities and your authority limits. This part sets your "utility" value. The other part deals with compensation, the salary and other perquisites that you will get. This part sets your "monetary" value.

Evaluating Job Content

Let us begin with your dream job. We have discussed this concept under "Your Dream Job" in chapter 2 earlier in this book. Now prepare a comparison table. List important job criteria in the leftmost column. In the next column, enter your expectations based on your dream job. In the next column, enter details from actual offers you have received.

In the last column, enter remarks as to how far the actual offers measure up to your target. You can indicate the match as a percentage. Thus, if the offer is actually better than what you had expected, you may rate it as, say, 110%. On the other hand, for some criterion, the offer may be no better than only 60 or 70% of your expectations. See the sample table later in this section.

It may appear a little difficult at first to quantify what are essentially qualitative measures such as job title. However, with a little thinking and analysis, you will find that it is indeed possible to compare your target with the offers.

Here is an example. Let us say that your target job description is "Regional manager". In one offer, the job description is "Product manager" and the other says, "Group supervisor". You may be able to rate the two at 90% and 70% after some thought.

TRAP Do not pay excessive attention to any single criterion. Organisations differ in nomenclature, so the same job may have different titles. However, if you use several appropriate criteria for comparing two or more offers to your target and to each other, you will get a fairly good idea as to which offer is better and nearer to your target.

Item	Target	Offer #1	Offer #2
Job Title	Regional Manager	Product Manager	Group Supervisor
Rating	100	90	70
Reporting to	General Manager	Group Manager	Regional Manager
Rating	100	75	80

Here are some job content criteria you could use in addition to the two shown in the sample table:

Item	Explanation
Job title	What will you be called?
Reporting to	Who is your boss?
Subordinates	Who reports to you? How many?
Prime responsibility	What will you do?
Authority limits	How much can you spend? What decisions can you take?
Travelling	How long and how often?
Shift work	Will you work in shifts?

The criteria given here are merely for illustration. If you have done sound information gathering as suggested under "Gathering Information" in chapter 2 earlier in this book, you should have no trouble in drawing up a set of criteria that suit you and the type of job you are seeking.

TIP

We suggest that you list the criteria in descending order of importance. For instance, if Job Title is more important to you than the person you report to, then list them as shown in the sample table. The offer scoring higher percentages in the top three or four criteria will probably be the one with the best job content.

Evaluating Monetary Content

Although money will probably exert more influence on your decision than the job content, we are discussing money second. There is a good reason for this. Money tends to overshadow other factors, probably more than it should. However, we urge you to take a long-term view of your career growth.

We are so heavily influenced by the salary amount that all other factors get pushed into the background.

TRAP Therefore, even though you should give money its due importance, it is better to first evaluate non-monetary aspects of competing job offers. You will get a more objective overall comparison of the offers thereby.

Evaluating the Total Package

Even when looking at monetary compensations, it is important to see the total package. In addition to salary, there are many other benefits such as a pension plan, provident fund and gratuity, medical insurance and several types of expense reimbursements amongst others.

Fresh graduates tend to devalue or overlook such benefits in the mistaken belief that retirement is too far in the future or health insurance is something they simply do not need.

NOTE Make sure that you evaluate all factors. If you have not received a formal compensation package along with the job offer, ask for it to be sent to you. If you are given the information verbally, take copious notes and ask clarifying questions on any areas you do not understand. In short, ensure that you evaluate every job offer based on hard facts and not assumptions and beliefs.

Evaluating Your Benefits Package

Benefits are not just for the twilight of your career. Usually, when we think of benefits we mean basic insurance coverage. However, a good benefit plan can include many additional perquisites. Let us examine some of the basic elements of benefit plans and what you should look for in them. Remember that each element may represent a negotiating opportunity.

General Insurance and Life Insurance Coverage

Find out who are covered from your family in addition to yourself. Some coverage may start from the day you join, others after the end of your probation period. Some others may come into effect only after you complete a year's service.

Medical Insurance

Check if it is a group policy or an individual policy. As in the case of general or life insurance, you should find out the effective date and the persons covered. Some policies may reimburse cost of consultation and medicines. Some others also cover hospitalisation. Check what diseases are excluded and what are the limits of reimbursement.

Accident and Disability Insurance

As in the case of other insurance policies discussed earlier, get full details. Disability insurance is usually divided into short-term disability (which can sometimes include sick pay) and long-term disability (which usually starts after six months to a year). Note the percentage amount, how that percentage may change over time, and what that percentage is based on.

Earned Leave

Consider how many days are allowed in your first year, when paid leave begins to accumulate, and when you can start using the leave. You may want to know, for instance, if you can claim leave in advance, before they are earned. Some companies do not provide any vacation during the first year. Check also whether vacation days accumulate according to the calendar year or work year based on your date of joining. You will also want to know the rules on accumulation, carry over and encashment of accumulated paid leave.

Paid Holidays, Casual and Sick Leave

Check your entitlement of paid holidays, casual and sick leave.

Provident Fund and Gratuity

The appropriate government authority generally regulates provident funds. However, there may be opportunity to choose a higher percentage of your pay as your contribution. The company will have rules regarding their matching contribution along with an upper limit. There is a minimum employment period to qualify for this benefit. Regarding gratuity, the company has greater discretionary powers and you should get details about percentages and minimum period of employment in order to qualify.

Pension Funds

While pension plans are often given little importance by young employees, it is an important consideration for security in later life. Do collect all relevant information.

Profit Sharing and Bonuses

Profit sharing and bonuses are very important benefits. Do note that while the amount of profit sharing could be at the discretion of executive management, in many cases, it is the outcome of collective bargaining between the organisation and the employees' union.

NOTE Since amounts can vary, ask what the company has paid, historically, for the last three years to individuals in a position similar to the one you are being offered. Get actual data and do not just accept promises that it is likely to be greater in the coming years. Because of the uncertainty involved, give less importance to bonuses when comparing two monetary offers.

Stock Options/ESOPs

These concepts are still new in India. In true stock options, you can opt to receive part of your compensation in the form of shares in the company. Alternatively, the organisation may have an Employee Stock Ownership Plan (ESOP). In this plan, you may buy company shares every year at a discount. Generally, these plans are rather risky for you if your employer is floating a new venture or is a new start-up company, since these share values may drop suddenly and very heavily.

Club Memberships

Some companies offer free or reduced-rate memberships in clubs. Some larger companies even offer on-site health club facilities so that you can work out in the morning, at lunch, or after work without having to leave the company premises.

Overtime/Compensatory Off

While salaried employees are usually not paid overtime, some companies will compensate for time above and beyond an expected standard (usually 44 or 48 hours per week). This can take the form of overtime or bonus pay, or compensatory days off.

Travel Expenses

These may be as a fixed allowance for daily travel to and from work. In addition, local and outstation business travel expenses may be reimbursed at some daily rate. Have all details and limits explained to you along with income tax implications, if any.

Business Expense Reimbursements

Organisations will usually reimburse living and entertainment expenses according to their rules, which will vary according to the position in the organisation. Some of these benefits may apply only to specialised employees such as sales personnel.

NOTE As we have mentioned before, the list of benefits is only for illustration. Your offer will contain only some of these and perhaps others not listed here. To evaluate the offers you receive, draw up a list that is appropriate for your case and use it for comparison and evaluation.

The Balance Sheet Technique

Suppose, after detailed analysis, you are still not sure. After all, the issue before you is vital for your future career. This is a situation that you may run into especially if you are a fresh graduate deciding on your very first job. There are two main reasons. Firstly, you have no past job parameters to compare with. Secondly, fresh job seekers apply to widely differing career opportunities so that the offers you receive will be very different from one another.

If you are in this situation, here is a final technique above and beyond the numbers and specifics to help you decide. It is called the "Balance Sheet Decision Technique". It is rumoured that Benjamin Franklin made frequent use of it to decide between alternatives!

BALANCE SHEET

FOR	AGAINST
1. Location	1. Work Hours
2. Pay	2. Work Conditions
3. Designation	3. No Car
4. Growth Prospects	4. Limited Authority

Begin by taking a sheet of paper. Draw a line down the middle. Then enter the heading "FOR" on the left side and "AGAINST" on the right side. Now begin to list the positive aspects of the offer on the left and the negative aspects of the offer on the right. Once everything is down on paper, the answer will usually become obvious to you.

NOTE When selecting the reasons for and reasons against, do not evaluate the position against your target job profile. Instead, evaluate it against the next best alternative. For some, that may be your present job. For others, it may be another job offer.

For some not-so-lucky ones, it may be continuing unemployment and job search.

TRAP Be very careful that you do not fall into a "hope trap", that is, comparing the offer you have in hand with another you hope will arrive soon. Until you have another firm, written offer in hand, you are really comparing an offer in hand with something that may only be in the air. Do remember the legendary saying about a bird in hand and ones in the bush!

NOTE If the job offer is still truly "unacceptable" according to the Balance Sheet Decision Technique, see the "Unacceptable Offer Negotiation" section in chapter 4 for advice on further action. Otherwise, what you have is really an "acceptable" job offer. You will, of course, want to make it better. To do so, read the "Acceptable Offer Negotiation" section in chapter 4 for advice on how to improve it.

Here is a graphic representation of the evaluation process...

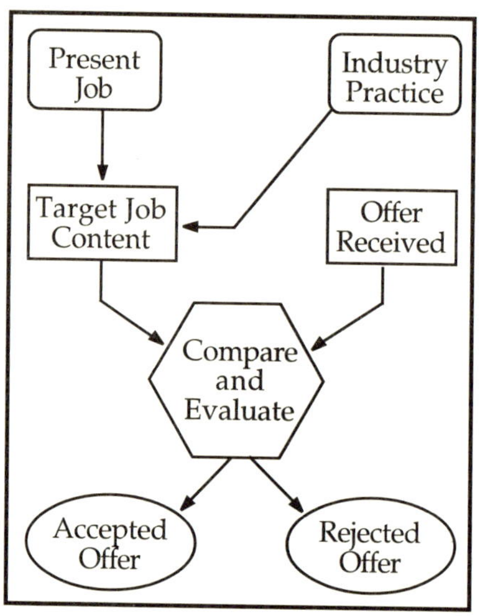

4 Negotiations

In this chapter:

- We discuss salary negotiation basics and negotiating strategy.
- The Noel Smith-Wenkle Method is explained to you.
- We describe how to handle unacceptable offers and improve acceptable ones.
- Take this self-test for evaluating your negotiating skills.

Yes! That is our absolutely final offer...
Until you refuse it! JLN

Salary Negotiation Basics

Congratulations! You have the coveted job offer in hand. You are now ready to negotiate your dream compensation package. You have prepared yourself and evaluated the offer as we have discussed in the previous two chapters. Now it is time to begin the actual negotiations. In this chapter, we go through the negotiation process with you. We begin with the basics.

Know Your Worth

You can be sure that the employer has a very clear idea of what the organisation is willing to pay for your services. They have a salary structure based on industry practice and they have assessed your qualifications and capabilities during the interviews.

NOTE In order to negotiate on a level playing field, you too must know what you are worth. We have discussed how you can assess your market value in chapter 2 earlier in this book. Knowing your worth helps you to set clear salary goals and a cut-off salary. Such clarity about your goal will give you confidence and greatly improve your chances of success.

A Clear Goal

Studies on negotiation consistently show that people who set clear and aggressive goals achieve more favourable settlements than those who aim low or do not set goals at all. It is important to have a target for salary and for the total compensation package. If you have set a target, you will be quick to respond decisively to any offer you receive.

A Cut-off Amount

Since you know your own financial goals, responsibilities and liabilities, you will also know what is the lowest offer you can accept. If the offer you receive is lower, it will not help your cause to pretend that you will take the offer. Do note, however, that your cut-off salary depends not only on your financial needs, but also on the alternatives you have, such as other offers, or your current job.

Emphasise Fairness

We often hear of the expression "a fair day's wage". The sense of fairness is very important for a "win-win" situation in which the employer and you can both feel satisfied when the negotiations end. The idea of fairness strikes a responsive cord in almost everybody, even though people have differing perceptions of what fairness exactly means to them.

TIP

Obtaining a compensation package that both you and the employer consider fair is particularly important since you are entering into an ongoing relationship. If you discover four months after taking the job that you are getting 20 per cent less than your counterparts, your morale will be badly damaged. On the other hand, if your employer feels that you had tricked them into a costlier package than the company's policy, they could easily become resentful towards you.

During negotiations, therefore, you should emphasise your special skills and experience so that the salary you want appears fair to the employer and commensurate with your worth to the organisation.

Identify Key Interests

Before you walk into the negotiation, prioritise your various interests and identify where you are willing to trade-off one thing of value for something else. For instance, is the salary more important than the pension plan for you? Would you rather get a club membership than a reduced period of probation?

When you negotiate the terms of the deal, try to explore what your employer's various interests and limitations are and reveal your own, but only what will benefit you.

TIP

Perhaps the employer cannot go above a certain salary and still maintain parity of salary within the company. However, in lieu of more salary, they may be able to offer stock options, other incentives, or a signing-on bonus instead. Be creative and flexible with your cut-off limits.

Compete but Cooperate

Try to match the style of the employer. If you face a tough negotiator, determined to bargain hard, it will not help your cause to be timid and to give in without a fight. This is where the concept of a cut-off salary is very useful. If the offer is much lower, say so clearly and firmly, without hesitation.

On the other hand, if your employer makes a concession, it is important that you also appear cooperative. You might need to make a concession as well.

TOP

Negotiating is not about winning at the other's cost. It is working towards a mutually acceptable goal. Therefore, each move you make will depend upon your goal as well as on the moves the employer makes.

Salary Negotiation Strategies

To the basic principles we have just discussed, let us now add a couple of tried-and-tested strategies that you can use in your own salary negotiations.

Negotiate the Job

If you are negotiating an entry level or a relatively low level job, try to upgrade the job content as you discuss your responsibilities. Point out how you can take on more responsibilities and contribute more to the organisation based on your own skills and qualifications. Make sure the employer agrees with the points you are making. Do not negotiate salary at this stage.

Outshine and Outlast Your Competition

To remain the last candidate standing in the field, you must be able to satisfy every legitimate need of the employer. Usually, this means surviving several levels of interviews. As you survive each stage, more competitors will drop out and your own bargaining strength will grow. Therefore, it is important to delay discussions on salary until the competition has been reduced and you are in a stronger bargaining position!

Handling Salary Requests

Picture this scenario: You have found the ideal job advertisement, but in the application form, they want you to give your salary expectations. Or, after the first interview, the human resources department asks you to forward your salary requirement and/or your salary history. What do you do?

NOTE Before we look at your options, let us examine why employers ask for your salary. Most often, the simple reason is that employers want an easy way to screen out applicants. They simply discard applicants whose salary expectations are either too low or too high. It is a part of the employer's strategy to save money by hiring a job seeker at the low end of a salary range. From your salary history, employers also want to see the frequency and size of increments and promotions. All this information strengthens the employer's bargaining position and does nothing for you! As you can see, all this is not really fair to the job seeker.

Your Market Value

What can you do about it? You do not wish to be screened out so early. At the same time, you do not wish to just give away information knowing that it may be used against you. So, prepare your response with care. As for salary history, always be truthful.

TOP

However, if you were underpaid in the past, do point this out in the covering letter. It will be very useful if you can point to any subsequent additional qualifications or experience that make you eligible now for a better salary.

Then, there is still the question of your salary requirement. Before you even think about answering it, you should do some research and make sure you know how much you are worth. See chapter 2 earlier in this book for details. We summarise here the key factors that contribute to your current market value.

Your Career Path

Regardless of what you have been paid in the past, spend some time reviewing industry reports of salary ranges for people in your career path, especially those working in comparable positions.

The Industry of the Employer

Salaries can vary, based on the industry of the employer. For example, companies in a service industry such as tourism often pay less than companies in a manufacturing industry requiring high technology.

The Geographic Location

The cost of living varies dramatically in different parts of the country. For example, it costs much more to live in Mumbai or New Delhi than it does in Kota or Thiruvananthapuram.

The Demand for Job-seekers

If there is a glut of job-seekers with essentially the same skills and experience that you have, you can expect salaries to be lower than if competing job-seekers are in short supply.

Some Answers You Can Use

TOP With a clear picture of your own market value, you will find it easier to respond to a request for your salary history and salary expectations. Here are some answers for your guidance:

1. In your covering letter, say that you expect a competitive/fair salary, or say that you are flexible about salary.
2. State that you prefer to discuss salary in an interview, but make sure to add that you do not think salary will be a problem.
3. Ignore the request for a specific salary expectation and simply show your salary history. Mention that you expect a reasonable increase on your current salary.

TRAP In these answers, since you have not given the employer your specific salary expectation, you do run a risk of being eliminated prematurely. To minimise this risk, select the second answer, seeking further discussions.

Whatever you decide, do not volunteer information about your salary history or your salary expectations or requirements in your covering letter, résumé, or during a job interview. Your objective should be to divulge your worth, not your past.

When to Expect a Request

Companies may ask you to disclose your current salary at any time during their interaction with you. We discuss the most likely situations and your recommended responses.

In the Advertisement for the Job

Some advertisements for jobs stipulate that candidates must disclose a salary history, a current salary, or a salary expectation in order to be considered for the job. Make sure that you stipulate in your covering letter that your salary expectation is the market value of the job.

In a Telephone Screening Interview

Before you set foot on company property, someone from the human resources office might screen you over the telephone and ask you to disclose your salary expectations or history. Companies do this to ensure that you are in the right salary range for them. You can set them at ease without committing to a number by saying, "I have researched the fair market value of this job. When we meet, I am confident we will find common ground."

During the Interview

Either a human resources representative or your potential future boss will ask you about your salary history as part of the interview. You should feel comfortable handling it in the same way as we have suggested earlier. Actually, salary requests are easier to handle in a face-to-face situation since you can observe the other's reaction to what you say and thus avoid any misunderstanding.

TIP

The organisation may push you hard for a detailed response. If so, come up with variations on the same answer. If you are changing your industry, you may point out, quite respectfully, that your old job does not compare with the new and, hence, past salary history is not really relevant. This is particularly true if you are switching from the public to the private sector. Try to deflect the salary question by focussing on what the new job requires and why the old pay would not be a good match for your increased duties and responsibilities.

The Smith-Wenkle Technique

It must be admitted that salary negotiation is something at which the employer's representative will be more proficient than the people they hire. After all, it is their profession. If you want to level the playing field, here is a method for salary negotiation to help you do so.

NOTE The technique is the brainchild of Noel Smith-Wenkle. A headhunter, he has been using this method for over two decades! You must remember that a headhunter's fees are proportional to the salary that the selected candidate gets, so it is in his interest to get the candidate the best possible salary package.

Noel Smith-Wenkle used this negotiation method for software developers in the Silicon Valley in the United States. However, in today's globalised marketplace, the technique will work equally well for you, right here in India!

Basic Assumptions

To save salary costs, almost all companies play a nasty little game. They ask you how much you want. Usually, there is a space on the application form named something like "Desired salary range". Since most of us automatically fill in all blanks on a form, we usually put down a figure.

NOTE Unfortunately, many people underestimate their own worth. If you are one of them, you will put down a low figure, less than what the organisation is prepared to pay. The organisation happily agrees to the figure you have put down. You are happy because you have got what you asked for (or nearly so), and they are happy because they are underpaying you and you are not likely to realise it.

TIP We have already advised you to have a minimum salary figure in mind before you begin negotiations. But this is strictly for your own information. It is not to be shared with the negotiator. Your purpose is to get the organisation to be the first party to name a number. If it is above your minimum, you accept. If it is too low, you tell them so, but you do not say by how much. They will either break off negotiations, or come back with a higher offer. Your responses should only be "okay" or "higher", never "X amount higher".

The Technique in Action

If you are asked to name a figure on the application form, leave it blank. Say in your covering letter that you would like to negotiate the salary face-to-face. Now you have a chance to get the organisation to disclose the opening bid. In an across-the-table negotiation, you can observe the negotiator's reaction to whatever you have to say. This will work to your advantage. When you do get the opportunity for a personal hearing, follow these three steps:

1. The first time you are asked your expected salary, reply:

"I am really more interested in doing (type of work) here at (name of organisation) than I am in the size of the initial offer." This sentence is constructed with great care. You may want to memorise it. By focussing on the job and not on the salary, you have set yourself apart from the other candidates, most of whom will disclose their salaries at this stage. Experts say that in about 40% of the cases, the hiring manager will make you a fair offer after your response. If they ask you again, take the second step.

2. The second time you are asked, reply:

"I will consider any reasonable offer." It lets you avoid the salary figure politely. At the same time, 'consider' and 'reasonable' leaves you with wide latitude. It is estimated that, after this reply, you will get a fair offer and it is necessary to go to step 3 only in 30% of the cases.

3. To the really persistent negotiator, asking your figure for the third time, say:

"By now, you are in a much better position to know how much I am worth to your organisation than I am."

NOTE Once again, you have been polite without naming a figure! You have also told them, at least by implication, that you are aware of their attempts to put pressure on you. Once you let them know that you recognise their tactics, these efforts to put you under pressure will stop and you will get a fair offer.

If you are indeed asked a fourth or even a fifth time, repeat step 3. However, this will very rarely happen. If it does, you may wish to reconsider joining an organisation that believes in playing games!

Handling Unacceptable Offers

Let us assume that the Smith-Wenkle technique has succeeded and you have the job offer. After you have evaluated it, you will have two situations on your hands. Either the offer is unacceptable in its present form or it is acceptable, but can be improved upon. The initial offer will rarely be a dream offer, far more than your best expectations. If indeed it is far in excess of your target, close this book and quickly accept it!

Tackle Unacceptable Offers First

We tackle unacceptable offers first as they are more likely to be rejected. So we should get them out of the way to concentrate on the better offers. If the offer is truly unacceptable, you must communicate this fact in no uncertain terms to the organisation. At the same time, you must keep the door open for negotiations. Here is an example of how you can respond:

"I am really very interested in working with you and your organisation. However (never use the word 'but'), at this point I am not able to accept the offer for the following reason." Now state your reasoning clearly and point out where the offer falls short of your expectation. Conclude by saying, "If you are able to meet my expectation (as mentioned), I will be glad to accept the job immediately. I believe that you can make this happen."

Your Strategy

It is important to be alive to the risks involved. First, you are putting the job offer at risk. In terms of contract law, you have just made a counteroffer, which technically rejects their initial offer. However, if the initial offer is truly unacceptable, you should be willing to accept this risk. Otherwise, you have no room for negotiation.

Second, you must clearly communicate what is specifically lacking in the initial offer. Is it the job title, the reporting level, the salary amount or some items in the perquisites package? By naming the shortfall quite specifically, you will reassure the organisation that while interested, you have a real problem with the offer.

Third, you must provide a specific solution. Tell them exactly what can be done to make things acceptable to you. Make it clear that only this specific shortfall is holding you back. Otherwise, you are ready to accept the offer on the spot.

Lastly, by saying that you believe that the negotiators have the power to grant your proposal you appeal strongly to their ego. If your proposal is reasonable and within the organisation's policy limits, there is a good chance of your getting what you want.

If Your Proposal is Turned Down

In spite of all your efforts if the organisation turns you down, try to understand the reason. Several factors may come into play.

For instance, a few organisations may have a rigid "first offer is last offer" policy. In other organisations, the entry-level salary structure may be quite rigid. If you find that they cannot adjust the salary under any circumstances, they will probably tell you so.

The problem may lie in the nature of your request. There may be restrictions based on designation levels that cannot be changed for you. For instance, a company car may only be given to vice-presidents. Be ready to consider alternatives, such as a suitable allowance for a car and driver.

NOTE Take into account the organisation's alternatives. If you are the only person in the world who can fill this position, they will probably make special concessions for you. If they have two others waiting in the wings, however, your bargaining position will not be as strong. If you have been listening carefully during interviews, you will probably become aware of the extent of competition and be able to adjust your bargaining strategy accordingly.

TIP Be aware of your bargaining strength and remain flexible. Seek alternatives actively if you run into resistance to your proposals. Be firm yet accommodative and, above all, be courteous and continue to show your interest in the job and in the organisation.

Follow these rules and your perseverance will pay off and, in many cases, you will convert an unacceptable offer into a satisfactory compromise.

Improving Upon Acceptable Offers

While there are clear-cut ways of tackling an unacceptable offer, it is actually more difficult to negotiate improvements to a "near acceptable" offer. The most important factor is psychological. If you know that the offer is much lower than what you are prepared to accept and it does not substantially improve in spite of your best efforts, you can turn your back on it with little regret.

But if the offer is close to your expectations, then you might be tempted to give in without much negotiation for fear of losing it altogether. Here, we outline a strategy for you to follow if the offer appears close to what you have in mind as a target.

Your Strategy

If you are negotiating with the one who will be your boss, the best approach for "sweetening" the job offer is to play upon the ego and power of your likely boss. The key to using this technique is to empower your would-be superior. You give him or her a feeling of power in two ways. Firstly by accepting the position you let him or her add a needed member to the team. Secondly, you make the boss feel powerful by asking for assistance in meeting your further needs.

How should you do this? Consider the following example:

NOTE Call up your would-be superior. Say that you are calling with some very good news. Say that you would like to accept the offer and that you are looking forward to working for him or her as a useful member of the team. Since you already see this person as your superior, you would much appreciate help to sort out a few small changes in the job offer. While it may or may not be within his or her direct authority area, you will greatly appreciate if he or she could look into it anyway.

Why Does it Work?

This technique ensures two things. First, it confirms your acceptance of the job. Thereby, your status changes from "one of the many" candidates to "the" candidate. Second, it narrows down the differences to small specific ones. If you have done a good job of convincing your interviewers that you are a very good candidate and willing to work for them, it is very likely that they will agree to a few small concessions to make sure that they add a willing and motivated member to their team.

The technique we have just discussed has a couple of major plus points. Firstly, it eliminates the chance of your being discarded as a candidate although you have asked for more than the initial offer. Therefore, you run no risk of losing the job. Secondly, you create a good rapport with your future boss by referring your request to him or her. It is very likely that he or she will add a few sweeteners to the initial offer.

NOTE Even if the boss is unable to do so at present, it is very likely that he or she will remember your unfulfilled request and take them into account while deciding increments or promotions in the future. Thus, you get an acceptable job offer plus the possibility of further future gains.

Do take note that we recommend this technique only if the initial offer be quite close to what you are ready to accept. If not, then you should use the strategy for negotiating unacceptable offers.

Negotiating Incentives and Benefits

We have discussed two negotiating scenarios in the previous sections. In both the cases, you may be told, "This is the absolute upper limit. We cannot offer you even a rupee more without upsetting our company salary structure."

The employer may well be right. There may indeed be no further room to bargain on the salary offered to you. But that does not mean that all negotiating options are now closed. You can explore two other facets of the compensation package, incentives and benefits. Let us look at them in detail.

Incentives You Can Negotiate

In addition to basic salary, you can discuss other incentives such as performance bonus, profit-sharing bonus, signing-on bonus, stock options, and similar benefits. You can also negotiate a relocation bonus if you are to move to a new location even if it is a new company owned or leased housing in the same city.

Instead of an increase in the salary offered, you can negotiate an accelerated performance review. You can ask for a shortening of your probation period and promise of a salary review after 3 months instead of the customary period of 6 to 12 months.

NOTE There are many other benefits that may attract you. They include healthcare benefits, opportunity for attending seminars and conferences, paid sponsorship to professional training courses, perhaps flexible working hours and a host of other possibilities. In addition to paid and casual leave, traditional benefits could include sick leave, short- and long-term disability cover, life insurance, accidental death and dismemberment insurance, survivor income, stock options, retirement plans, and many more.

TIP At the end of your first interview, especially if the interviewer is from the company's human resources department, ask about benefits offered by the organisation. While you may negotiate your salary with whoever is interviewing you, the human resources (HR) person is the best source of information on incentives and benefits.

Test Yourself

Congratulations! You have just completed a vital chapter. Your salary negotiation skills should now be at its peak. How would you like to test yourself? Take this easy True/False test to see how well you have picked up our advice. You will find the answers in the Annexure at the end of this book.

True or False?

Your time limit is 10 minutes.

1. Your "qualifications" and "performance" will automatically determine your salary level.

   True ☐ False ☐

2. When asked, "What are your salary requirements?" give no reply.

   True ☐ False ☐

3. You should calculate tangible and intangible benefits as part of the compensation package.

   True ☐ False ☐

4. You should not state a specific salary expectation figure on your job application form.

   True ☐ False ☐

5. Almost all employers predetermine the salaries they will offer.

   True ☐ False ☐

6. You should never negotiate salary and benefits over the telephone.

   True ☐ False ☐

7. If the initial offer you receive is a good one, accept it on the spot.

   True ☐ False ☐

8. The gross salary figure is more important than individual benefits in a salary package.

   True ☐ False ☐

9. It is easier to negotiate if the initial offer is very close to being acceptable by you.

   True ☐ False ☐

10. You should negotiate salary based on your financial needs.

True ☐ False ☐

Now look at the expert's answers in the Annexure at the conclusion of this book. Apart from the correct answers, you will find reasoning to support the right answer. Study the reasoning to get additional tips on negotiations.

How did you do? If you did well, that is wonderful! Move on to the next chapter. If too many answers did not come out right, do not worry! Just read the chapter over again.

5 Closing the Deal

In this chapter:

- How to bring the negotiations to a close with good timing and grace.
- How to make your final commitment and create the right atmosphere for entry into the new organisation.
- How to deal with counteroffers that you may receive from your old organisation.
- A final quiz, we help you to decide if you are ready.

You have two choices, resign or jump! JLN

Importance of Closing the Deal

Shortsighted salespeople focus on just closing the sale. Successful salespeople focus both on making a sale and maintaining a long-term relationship with the customer. You face a very similar situation when you are closing a job offer negotiation. You may focus only on the best possible salary package for yourself, or you can also take into account the importance of continuing a good relationship with your employer.

TIP Your relationship with your employer will be longer and closer than the one between a salesperson and a customer whom he may never see again. Therefore, a good closure is of vital importance to your future success at your job.

How do you know that it is time to close? Your interviewer may indicate closure by saying, "This is our final offer and no further discussion is possible." While this is one way to find out that the negotiations are over, you really do not want to end on such a hostile note.

TRAP Unfortunately, such an ending does not mean that you have bargained successfully and you are about to emerge as the only winner. Instead, it shows the interviewer's exasperation with your tactics and is really an ultimatum. Even if you accept the offer and join the organisation now, you have started off the relationship on the wrong foot.

You should end the negotiations at a stage when both you and the employer feel that each has got some benefit out of it. You have secured a good job at a good salary and the organisation has gained a valuable member for the team.

NOTE A successful negotiation must end in a win-win situation. If not, all your efforts, begun with your job application, interviews and salary negotiations, will fail to bear fruit. Therefore, the art of closing the negotiations is vital. Your success will depend on what may be called your closing philosophy or attitude. Let us examine this important aspect.

A Good Closing Philosophy

A closing attitude or philosophy says, "I am here because I can be a useful employee for the organisation. I am here because I want to work for you. I am not here because I am highly qualified or I have an unsurpassed track record of success." In other words, you emphasise your usefulness and worth to the potential employer.

TIP

Your focus is on your qualifications and experience, but not in isolation. Take pains to explain how your education fits in with the job needs and how your past experience is exactly what will help the organisation to succeed and grow.

If you have researched the organisation and the job and then prepared for the negotiations, you will be able to make the connection between what the organisation wants and what you can offer as a candidate. In that sense, your job interview will carry into the salary negotiations as a continuation. You have to negotiate money and display your worth to the employer at the same time.

TOP

While you will keep an eye on money, miss no opportunity for showing how good the fit is between the job needs and your skills. With this approach, you will meet less resistance to your counteroffers or additional demands. They will appear justified because you are such a good candidate. This is the key to bring the negotiations to a win-win conclusion rather than an ultimatum from the employer as we saw earlier.

Successful closing of negotiations is not something that begins at some magical point in time. It is the outcome of your sustained efforts and maintenance of the right attitude throughout the salary negotiation.

Check Your Attitude

Since the right attitude is so important for success, how do you ensure that you maintain it all along? This checklist will help you. Constantly ask yourself:

1. Am I focussing on how I can be of value to the organisation?
2. Am I being able to demonstrate how my qualifications and experience fit the job requirements?
3. Are there any concerns or reservations that the interviewer has about me? If so, how far have I been able to address these concerns?
4. Why should the organisation hire me? Have I been able to find at least one unique talent of mine that the organisation needs?

TOP Check your negotiating style frequently to make sure that it is on track. If you focus exclusively on monetary bargaining, the negotiation will become confrontational. Bring matters back in focus and revive the win-win formula by using one or more of the checkpoints given above.

Close Gracefully

If you can keep the atmosphere co-operative, then after you and the employer have both made some concessions, you will find a satisfactory middle ground. When that happens, accept the offer promptly with genuine grace and gratitude.

TOP Now is the time to drop your guard. As you accept the final offer, your status changes. Suddenly, instead of sitting on two opposite sides of the bargaining table, you move to the same side as your interviewer and you become team members. Show that you are truly glad to join the team.

Your Final Commitment

After accepting the negotiated offer, you are ready to make your final commitment to the new organisation. It should be a sincere commitment that you are willing to stand behind. Organisations spend money, use resources, and draw up their business plans based on your promise to join. They may also inform unsuccessful candidates that the position has been filled. So make sure that you are willing to honour your commitment before you make it.

After committing yourself to the new organisation, you will still be left with a couple of clean-up type of jobs. We discuss these one by one.

Counteroffers

It is quite likely that if you are already employed, your current employers will try to retain you. They may try to persuade you not to leave. They may even make a counteroffer with promises to match the salary and benefits you have been promised in your new job.

TOP

If you have carefully compared the new offer with your current job (including your immediate increment and promotion prospects) it should be obvious to you that you should not accept any counteroffers.

We will discuss in detail the reasons why you should reject it and our advice on handling the situation later in this chapter.

Give Proper Notice

If you have selected the right job for a career move and have negotiated well, your new job will be both exciting and financially rewarding. It is natural for you to want to move to it right away. But even if the position is vacant, no ethical employer should ask an already employed person to start immediately. It is just not done. Even if you are not happy with your current employer, you owe them the professional courtesy of giving proper notice.

NOTE The normal notice period is one month. You may refer to the terms and conditions of your existing job and find out what is the notice period you are bound to give. In certain circumstances, you may be able to persuade your current employer to reduce your mandatory notice period. If you have privilege leave due, you may convince your employer to agree to deduct the leave days from the notice period.

If you are in-charge of something important and no understudy is ready to take over, your present employer may request you to extend your notice period beyond one month.

TIP While you should part with grace and goodwill, it is never good strategy to extend your time with the current employer and defer the date of joining your new employer. Once you accept a new job offer, you switch your loyalties. Your place is in the new organisation. Therefore, as soon as you can, make the transition.

Handling Counteroffers

We have mentioned counteroffers earlier. While changing jobs, this is a major dilemma that many have to face. Let us look at the situation closely.

Why Counteroffers are Made

If you are currently employed and ready to move on to your new employer, the time has come to tell your current boss that you are leaving. For your boss, however, it is probably not a good time for you to leave. There are many reasons. You may be in-charge of something important and it is not yet finished. The organisation may have prepared no successor for your position. Or, the boss simply does not want to go through a lengthy replacement process. Whatever the reason, your organisation wants to retain you. So, they make a counteroffer in order to induce you to stay.

NOTE Companies concerned with the best interests of the employees rarely make counteroffers. Only those companies that place their corporate interests ahead of your personal interests are likely to do so. If your boss is convinced that you are making a really good career move, he or she should actually encourage you to go ahead. However, for reasons we have just seen, the boss may be thinking of himself or herself rather than you!

So the boss breaks into the "I did not realise you were unhappy here" speech and begins probing you to find why you are leaving. "More money? Higher position? More perks? We will offer you the same or a better position if you will stay!" Does it appear too good to be true? Actually, that is exactly what it is.

TRAP The only reason why the counteroffer is being made is because your boss wants to choose the time he or she wants you to leave. The boss may need time only so that you can finish that important project, or they can find a replacement. Once that happens, you will find that you are no longer wanted and at that time, you will no longer have that attractive job offer in your hand!

Yet many people accept counteroffers. The reason is that the counteroffer gives us the benefits of the new offer with the comfort of staying right where we are. But there are several fallacies in that line of thinking. First, the reasons for leaving still exist—some of those reasons may be temporarily altered by the counteroffer, but they are still there. Second, you are offered what you deserve only when you are leaving! Third, and most important, by accepting the counteroffer, you lose control over your destiny and hand it over to your present employer.

TIP

Remember that the counteroffer has nothing to do with the employer's "loyalty" to you or any other emotion. It is strictly a business deal. At the first opportunity to replace you, your head will roll because the employer no longer trusts your "loyalty" to them. The money spent on you due to the improved terms of the counteroffer is usually less than what will be needed to hire and train an understudy immediately. Therefore, as we said, the counteroffer is strictly business and always temporary.

What You Should Do

TOP

Here is the best course of action if and when a counteroffer is made. Just smile and say "Boss, I am flattered that you consider me important and would like to keep me as part of the team. But I have made up my mind. I have made my commitment and I will be leaving as soon as my notice period is over. Please tell me what I can do to make the transition as smooth as possible and I shall be happy to co-operate."

Even if you reject the counteroffer, you may still expect several attempts to delay your departure. You may be asked to wait till some important work is finished or till a replacement is found and trained. Your loyalties are now with your new employer and you should not delay taking up your new responsibility to accommodate your existing employer. Your stay should not exceed beyond your notice period.

TIP

Remember, under no circumstances should you give in to a counteroffer, no matter how tempting it may seem. Consider delaying your date of departure only under extreme circumstances and only after you are sure that the delay in joining is acceptable to your new employer.

Separating Gracefully

No matter how difficult your previous employer was, no matter how terrible your boss was, no matter how evil your co-workers were, never ever burn your bridges behind you! Regardless of what your problems were and whatever grievances you may have, do not take it out on your boss or co-workers in person. A defiant or vindictive attitude will get you absolutely nothing except a very temporary feeling of superiority.

TIP

Even if you were treated unfairly, do not sink to their level in order to "get even". The most respectable thing you can do, especially when you have had a difficult time; is to leave with honour and dignity. Keep your head up and keep your mouth shut. You will leave with respect instilled in your character rather than disgust instilled in your heart.

Here is a true story of how a burned bridge came back to haunt a man who changed jobs. He felt that he had every right to tell his boss exactly what he thought of him, and did just that. Imagine his shock and horror when this former boss was hired by his new company some two years later, and became his new boss! Needless to say, our hero lasted only a few months before he was forced to change jobs once again!

NOTE

The professional world is much smaller than you think. People in the same business know each other and people talk. People you hurt can find ways of damaging your careers even when you no longer work for the same organisation. Conversely, cool and professional conduct is praised and appreciated. Your conduct while you work and when you leave will decide if your reputation grows as you progress in your profession. So try to remain calm and in control of yourself at all times.

Look forward, not backward. If you really want to surprise your tormentors in your previous job, sincerely

thank them for all the help they have given you. Do your very best work in the time you remain with the organisation, and make them realise what a gem they are losing!

The Final Test

In chapter 4 you have already encountered a quiz designed to give you a feedback on how well you have understood the negotiation process. In this section, we have another quiz for you. It is a more general test covering other chapters as well. Take this test to gauge your overall understanding of the salary negotiation process. If you do well, it will boost your morale. If you do not, it is better that you get the warning now, so that you have time to read this book once again!

Answers with explanations are given in the Annexure. Tick what you think is the most appropriate answer. You should be able to complete the test in 20 minutes.

1. To negotiate effectively, I must conduct sufficient amount of research to know what I am worth in the marketplace based on my experience, skills, education, and geographic location.

   True ☐ False ☐

2. To get the best salary offer, I need to prove my value to the company in a way that highlights my skills and abilities over all other job-seekers.

   True ☐ False ☐

3. A good starting point for salary negotiations for a new job is to aim for at least a 20 per cent increase over my current salary.

   True ☐ False ☐

4. If I think the employer will make an offer and I want this job, then I should raise the salary question first.

   True ☐ False ☐

5. For the company, industry, and type of job I have applied for, at the interview, I should have a clear idea of the exact range of salary and types of benefits I want.

   True ☐ False ☐

6. I should avoid giving direct answers to salary requirements or salary history if I am asked such questions early in the interviewing process.

   True ☐ False ☐

7. When the employer raises the issue of salary or compensation during the interview, it is a clear indication that the company is interested in making me an offer.

   True ☐ False ☐

8. During the interview, if the employer makes an offer that is acceptable to me, I should accept it on the spot to show my commitment to the company.

   True ☐ False ☐

9. I should always request getting the job offer in full detail. The entire compensation package in writing should be in my hands before I make a final decision.

   True ☐ False ☐

10. It is almost always possible to negotiate some aspect of a job offer. If not salary, then other compensation, benefits or incentives can be negotiated.

    True ☐ False ☐

11. Salary negotiations are a gamble. It is really all part of a game that employers and job-seekers play.

    True ☐ False ☐

12. Even if the job I am offered is my dream job, if the salary offer is below my minimum acceptable amount, I should decline the offer.

    True ☐ False ☐

13. If the employer makes an unacceptable job offer, I should be prepared to begin negotiations immediately.

    True ☐ False ☐

14. If the negotiations seem at a standstill over one or more compensation issues, I should give the employer an ultimatum to finish the negotiations quickly.

    True ☐ False ☐

15. After accepting the employer's original offer, it is still possible for me to negotiate a better compensation package.

    True ☐ False ☐

16. I need to be a master negotiator to really get the salary I want.

    True ☐ False ☐

17. During negotiations, I should always try to judge when it is time to stop bargaining and end the negotiations.

    True ☐ False ☐

18. If I have two or more job offers, it is a good idea to encourage all my prospective employers to compete with each other by telling each of them what the others have offered me.

    True ☐ False ☐

19. If the salary offer is near the minimum I will accept, and I am told that the offer is not negotiable, I should consider asking for a "signing-on" bonus as an alternative.

    True ☐ False ☐

20. If the employer sets a time limit for my acceptance, I can safely exceed the limit before taking a final decision.

True ☐ False ☐

21. If I have more than one job offer in hand, the offer with the highest starting salary is always the best choice.

True ☐ False ☐

6 Starts, Raises and Appraisals

In this chapter:

- ➢ We address the special concerns of fresh entrants to the job market.
- ➢ Appraisals form the basis of salary reviews. We discuss how to prepare for them.
- ➢ We discuss your strategies to make sure you get top salary reviews every year in your current job.

Introduction

In this book so far, we have addressed all of those who are about to negotiate a new job offer package. While we have not specifically said so, we have targeted people who have negotiated salary before. We believe we have helped them to sharpen their skills and do better than the last time.

Even for veterans of many negotiations, the experience is emotionally draining and mentally taxing. It is easy to imagine, therefore, how much more difficult negotiations will be for the fresh graduate, the new entrant to the job market, one with hopes and fears but no past experience to fall back upon.

The needs of the new players are indeed different from others, whether it is their first salary negotiation, their first participation in a performance appraisal or the very first annual salary review. We address these needs in this chapter.

NOTE While the focus is on our young readers, these tips, be it for better increments or more satisfying performance appraisals, will apply to everybody. So, even if you are a seasoned veteran, do read what we have to say. We are sure that you too will be able to pick up a valuable pointer or two.

Guidelines for Fresh Graduates

Salary negotiation is a disturbing emotional experience. You want the job, but you also want to be paid what you are worth. The offer seems low and yet you hesitate to be assertive. The problem is, you are new to this and have no past experience of putting a monetary price on your services.

You are not sure how you can justify a higher salary or improved fringe benefits as a fresh graduate since you have little or no experience.

NOTE The answer lies in understanding the negotiation process better. With a clearer understanding of how to go about it, you will feel more in control during the negotiations and more comfortable with the outcome even if it is not as good as you had hoped for.

Understand the Process

Let us start with a definition of what a negotiation is. In your case, it is meeting and discussing your salary and benefits with another person in order to reach an agreement. The art of negotiation is based upon mutual agreement of issues, not confrontation. This is an important point. For those new to negotiations, it is easy to either become too timid or too aggressive.

NOTE While formal salary negotiation usually begins after the interview process, it really starts right from the initial interview. Your worth to the organisation and hence the salary they will want to pay you is determined by your accomplishments and your capacity to do what the employers want you to do.

Therefore, what you tell the company about yourself, your qualifications and your relevant experience has a direct bearing on your value to them. If you do it right, when the time to offer you a job comes, you will get a good offer.

TOP Use active words in the interview to describe your accomplishments such as: I initiated, I oversaw, I created, I took charge of, I followed up on, I actively contributed to, and I developed. The ability to handle details, multiple projects or excellent time management and follow-up skills will also contribute to your value. If you do so, you are already negotiating for a good salary long before money has been mentioned!

Get the Facts!

Negotiating is not merely saying, "I want more money." To negotiate with authority, you must collect information and have some clear ideas. Here are three areas for you to investigate along with possible information sources:

1. What is the salary range of the job with the employer and/or the industry that I am planning to join?

Your seniors who are already employed, friends and relatives who work in that industry, libraries, web sites on the Internet and business magazines are sources that you must tap for answers to this question.

2. What is the lowest salary that I will consider?

You must set up a realistic "walk-away" price for yourself. Use the track record of the last year's batch as a guide for determining your minimum expectations.

3. What makes me worth a higher salary?

Recall your academic performance, your extra-curricular activities, also instances when you led with distinction or excelled in an academic subject to draw up your own chart of excellence.

Fine-tune Your Mindset

Even if you know the answers to these questions, you will still have to face negative comments such as:

- You do not have enough experience.
- Other employees are not getting as much as you have asked.
- Our budget will not permit it.
- Well! That is all we pay fresh graduates.

Think about how you would respond to these objections. You want the discussions to continue on a positive note without becoming confrontational. Remember to ask questions or make suggestions, not deliver an ultimatum.

TOP

For example in responding to the "Other employees are not getting as much as you have asked" statement, you may use a response such as: "I see... (A small pause.) What is the salary range for this position? What qualities are you looking for in the candidate who will deserve a higher point in that range?" This will open the discussion further and give you an opportunity to point out that you do indeed possess the very qualities that the organisation wants.

Ask a few questions to see if there might be a way to accommodate each other's point of view. Always remember that you are looking for a convergence of interests and not trying to score debating points. It is important to remember that fresh graduates are hired on a tight budget.

TIP

If you want to break the standard offer barrier, you have to give some compelling reasons. One thing that may help you stand out from the competition is evidence that you have researched your facts in detail and that you have a mature negotiating style.

The Interview

As we have said, salary negotiations start right from the time you appear for your very first interview. Therefore, keep these thoughts in mind during all interviews:

1. Listen carefully so that you understand the needs of the company and the individual interviewing you. Your replies should focus on demonstrating how you are in a position to meet these needs, through your education, and your "can-do" attitude.

2. Good listening is more than simply not interrupting and allowing the interviewers to finish their thoughts. Repeat back key points you hear to reassure your interviewer that you are paying full attention. Establish good eye contact and nod after a statement

to confirm that you have heard it. More positive body language tips are given in the next section.

3. Try not to be the first one to mention money. You must get an indication of what the organisation is prepared to offer you before showing your hand.

TOP

If asked directly about your salary expectations, answer that you expect a competitive offer and bring the discussion back to your value as an employee. If you are already employed and you are asked what your current pay is, tell the truth. However, if you are due for an increment soon, mention that also.

Body Language

You may not realise it, but unknowingly, you may convey your thoughts, doubts and fears to your interviewer. If you do not pay attention, what you convey through your body language may be negative, even contradictory to what you say. Pay attention to your body language, therefore, so that your well-prepared answers do not fail to convince your interviewers. Here are a few simple rules:

1. Avoid staring hard, a defiant shake of the head or a pointing or wagging finger. All these gestures suggest aggression. Disagree pleasantly. Maintain a neutral, relaxed posture and a friendly tone in your voice.

2. Avoid defensive body language such as arms folded across your body or crossed legs. These gestures signify that you are rigid in your thinking and not open to suggestions.

3. Do not stare, but do look the interviewer in the eye when you are making an important point. If your eyes slide away as you speak, it will give you a furtive look and cast unfounded doubts on your reliability.

NOTE Be comfortable and relaxed. While you do want to appear alert and attentive, do not give the impression of being tense or desperate for the job. Interviewers will sometimes put the candidate under pressure to gauge their ability to handle stress. What you say and how you say it will show how well you can handle a difficult situation.

The Offer

Here is how to respond to a job offer:

1. If you receive an acceptable offer say that you are very interested and excited about the opportunity. Say that you will get back to them in a day or two since you need time to carefully study the offer.
2. Once the base salary has been discussed, but before accepting the job, ask them about the other important fringe benefits you might be entitled to. Usually, the HRD department of the organisation will be able to give you full details.
3. Avoid telephone negotiations. It is very important to be able to observe the reactions of the other party when negotiating.

The Negotiation

Tricky situations may arise during negotiations. Keep these tips in mind. They may help you out of a tight corner:

1. During negotiations, frame your counteroffers as a question rather than a flat statement. A question does not sound like a demand and therefore will not antagonise the interviewer. Here is an example:

TOP Interviewer: "The starting salary is Rs. 8,000.00 per month."

You: "I am delighted that you are interested in me. I am very eager to join the organisation. Since my place of work is far from my parent's home, I intend to live on my own and I estimate that I will need a minimum of Rs. 10,000.00 per month to meet all my expenses and to save a little. Is there some way you can help me to meet my salary goal?"

2. If the job is attractive but the salary structure is rigid, ask if it is possible to have the probation period reduced to 3 or 6 months. You should qualify for a review and a salary increment after probation.

3. If you are able to agree on the main salary structure, you can usually gain additional concession by showing your desire to join, but for "one small thing".

TOP

You can say something like: "I am generally satisfied with your offer. I am looking forward to the opportunity to contribute to the organisation. I can make a commitment right now only if we can find a way to solve one little problem." Then state specifically what you want.

TIP

In summary, remember that you will spend the next 40 to 50 years working. Therefore, it is important that every time you look for a job, settle for one that you like and for which you are qualified. If you get an offer from a reputed company with a great future potential, then the immediate salary is less important than your future career prospects. Accept the offer even if the salary is lower than what you have wished for.

Pay attention to these simple negotiating principles and not only will your salary packages be attractive, but your career will also blossom. Good luck!

Performance Review

So far, we have been concentrating on salary negotiations that follow job offers. Unless you change jobs every year, these negotiations are infrequent. In a working life of 40 years or so, the average employee will go through such negotiations anywhere between 4 to 8 times. However, the same employee will face performance appraisals and salary reviews every year.

For job satisfaction and career growth, you have to make sure that you prepare for and take part effectively in your performance reviews. Since your increments and promotions will depend on your performance, it is vital for you to make sure that these reviews are favourable.

NOTE Take careful note that the key is not just how you perform, but how you are seen to perform by others, especially your boss. Because your boss's perspective is so critical, you must train yourself to observe your own performance from his or her point of view. Admittedly, this is not easy.

TRAP Most of us believe that virtue is its own reward. If we are doing a good job, we should automatically be rewarded. Therefore, if the annual reward is not what we expect, we get upset, feel betrayed and may lose motivation to work hard. The outcome is that we achieve even less the next year and hence earn a reprimand instead of a reward. The cycle continues and our career gets worse and worse.

To break out of this vicious cycle, we must learn to gauge our performance and take corrective action in an objective manner, observing our actions as our manager will see it.

TOP Let us take an example. When assigned a task, you may do a fine, meticulous job. However, because of the time you take to be meticulous, the job finishes too late. You may expect a reward for the quality of work done while you actually get a reprimand because the deadline is well past. On another occasion, as a team member, you get a project finished ahead of time, but antagonise the rest of the team by claiming all credit. You see only the completion date and expect a reward but get reprimanded because of the disharmony you bring to the team.

Some Ground Rules

Here are some ground rules to ensure that your performance appraisal is favourable:

1. Compare your performance with the agreed performance targets. To what extent did you achieve them?

2. Have you taken on any additional responsibilities or been involved in extra projects? How have you dealt with changes, innovations or unexpected problems? Are there ways in which you can increase your value to the organisation?

3. Keep a detailed record of your work-related activities throughout the year. Specify your contributions and achievements, your difficulties and frustrations. Ensure that all relevant facts and figures are accurate and readily accessible. Collect necessary documentary evidence to support your assertions. Make a list of all conferences, seminars and training courses you have attended.

4. Be open and co-operative with your reviewer. Acknowledge problems, and deal positively and maturely with criticism. Do not become defensive.

5. If you are unhappy about targets or feel that they are unrealistic, say so as tactfully as possible.

TIP

To document your contribution to the company, keep a job diary. Your first day on the job is a good time to start. Make a habit of writing down what you did and how it helped meet the company's objectives. Anticipate the future by thinking about what you would like to accomplish next year and keep a record of your thoughts.

6. Think seriously about what your general behaviour conveys to those around you. Try to be "likeable" in the corporate sense. That means being pleasant and respectful to others, and deferential to people with

more experience. It means being comfortable with the organisation's rules and willing to put in extra work when it is called for.

NOTE Although a performance review is usually separate from salary or promotion reviews, the two are closely related. A good performance review will earn you increments in salary and two or three good reviews in a row will almost certainly earn you a promotion.

Negotiating a Salary Increase

We have just seen how good performance appraisals will lay the foundation for salary increases and promotions. Sometimes, however, your career may need a special push. If you feel that your good performance is not being adequately rewarded in the form of salary increase, here is some advice about what to do:

- ❑ If you believe you deserve a salary increase, ask for it as soon as possible; do not procrastinate or wait for your employer's offer.
- ❑ Before you ask for a salary increase, determine what you are worth in the marketplace by carrying out a survey of people in comparable jobs. Never base your case on your need for more money.

NOTE

- ❑ Be realistic in your assessment of what you are worth and what your employer would be willing or able to pay. Have an exact figure in mind before entering into negotiations. Always avoid comparisons with your colleagues. Never justify your request based on someone else's increment or promotion.

TOP

- ❑ Remember that bosses want employees who contribute to the company's success by: increasing sales, profits and efficiency; decreasing waste, costs and time taken;

improving corporate image, customer relationships and competitive advantage. Your request for a salary increase must be based on what you have actually achieved in these areas, not on what you think you can do.

- ❑ Carry out a detailed analysis of your job description. Be as objective as you can, identifying specific ways in which the company has benefited from your skills, qualifications, work, and experience. These are valid grounds for seeking a salary increase.
- ❑ When preparing for a performance review, anticipate difficult questions by identifying weaknesses in your case. Be prepared with positive answers.

NOTE

- ❑ If you have records of recent appraisals, study them carefully highlighting your achievements and indicating how you have addressed any shortcomings. If you have overcome past weaknesses, it will be a strong argument in your favour.
- ❑ Negotiating skills are very important. Listen carefully to what your boss is saying. Do not be confrontational under any circumstances. Avoid ultimatums and be prepared to compromise if necessary.
- ❑ If, because of circumstances beyond his or her control, your boss feels unable at this time to give you an increment, thank him or her for listening and request another salary review within three months.

Remember that you will have to work with your boss in the future. So, regardless of the outcome of the meeting, leave on good terms, and do not bang the door behind you!

Annexure: Answers to the Quizzes

Chapter 4

1. **FALSE.** Employers set their initial offer at the mid-point of the salary range for the job they want to fill. Your qualifications and experience will help you to get a better offer (but within the range) only if you explain your usefulness to the employer in terms of the organisation's needs. The employer will not automatically offer you the best salary you deserve.

2. **FALSE.** You cannot avoid the question. Respond by saying that you are more interested in the opportunities that the job has to offer than salary and that you are open to a reasonable and competitive offer.

3. **TRUE.** Even intangible benefits, ones that cannot be translated into money, should be taken into account. For instance, if the organisation has a gymnasium in the office premises, although it is not a monetary benefit, it may be a long-term benefit for your health and well-being.

4. **TRUE.** Unfortunately, this advice is often forgotten. Most of us tend to fill all the blanks in a job application form fearing that our application may be rejected otherwise.

5. **FALSE.** See the answer to question 1 above.

6. **TRUE.** It is very important that you only negotiate face-to-face. It is essential that you are able to observe the reaction to your responses and, thereby, modify your negotiating strategy as the interview progresses.

7. **FALSE.** It is very important that you give yourself time to study all aspects of the offer, and compare it to your present compensation or to another offer you already have. Ask for some reasonable time for your response.

8. **TRUE.** Although some benefit may be very desirable in your eyes, the organisation is also bound by its rules. Be flexible and be ready to trade off between benefits, keeping an eye on the total.

9. **FALSE.** If the offer is already good, you will tend to accept immediately because you may not want to risk that your counteroffer is rejected. However, if you accept right away, you may miss an opportunity for further negotiations. To play safe, you can accept the offer and make a request for some additional (and specific) concessions.

10. **FALSE.** The employer will pay according to your worth to the organisation and not according to your needs.

Chapter 5

1. **TRUE.** Knowledge and information are the absolute power bases in salary negotiation. This is why employers always try to determine your salary history and/or salary demands before making their offer. Take time to research salary levels, not only by job title, but also by industry, by geographic location, by level of demand for job-seekers with your skills. Study the company's salary practices as thoroughly as possible.

2. **TRUE.** This strategy should be your goal all the time you are job-hunting. It is important to show that you are uniquely qualified for the position. The higher your potential value in the eyes of the interviewer, the better will be the job offer you will receive.

3. **FALSE.** Because salary is often the main cause for a job change, it is easy to be blinded by the desire for a specific increase in pay and make this the sole criterion for your decision. This strategy often fails because what you seek may be a much higher percentage than what the typical employer awards in annual increments. Instead, you should look beyond your current salary and focus on the long-term opportunities of the job being offered.

4. **FALSE.** The longer the salary discussion is delayed, the better is your bargaining power. You can negotiate a better package if you are the last candidate in the employer's list and the others have been eliminated. However, you must be prepared for the salary discussion to arise at any time in the interview process. It is important to remember that some employers take offence when a job-seeker appears money-hungry by asking about salary too early in the interview process.

5. **TRUE.** We cannot overstress the rewards you will reap from a thorough salary research early in your job search. Each job and each company will have a

different mix of salary ranges and benefits, depending on a number of factors. You really need to know these factors and know what to expect, what to negotiate, and what to accept.

6. **TRUE.** Employers ask about salary history and salary requirements because that is how they conduct their research on you. They want to know what you have got in the past and what you expect to get now. Try to delay any and all salary negotiations until the very end by avoiding these types of discussions. Be very careful, however, since ignoring the employer's request may lead to your being dropped as a candidate. Experts suggest masking your specific salary requirements by saying that "you expect competitive or fair compensation" or that your salary request is "flexible".

7. **FALSE.** Interviewers simply raise the issue of salary to test your reaction and try and gain valuable information about you.

8. **FALSE.** No matter how attractive the offer, it is always better to set it aside for some length of time and then review the offer objectively, away from the stare or glare of the interviewer. Once you have accepted the offer, you have no scope of further negotiations. Therefore, accept only after due consideration and only after you are convinced that there is no further room for negotiations.

9. **TRUE.** All reputable employers want you to have full information about a job compensation package before you make your final decision. It is not in their interest that you should become disgruntled and demoralised if you find the reality less than your expectations, after joining. Be extremely wary of prospective employers who refuse to give you the complete offer in writing. If that happens, write a follow-up letter to the employer outlining the

compensation package, as you understand it and asking specifically for all the missing items.

10. **TRUE.** A majority of employers are flexible on at least some elements of the compensation package – even if salary is not negotiable. On the other hand, only a small percentage of job-seekers actually try and negotiate a better job offer. No doubt, there is some inherent risk in trying to negotiate with an employer who is rigid, but even in those situations the offer is rarely withdrawn. Just be sure you know the key rules of negotiating, as outlined in this book.

11. **FALSE.** One of the worst mistakes a job-seeker can make is to think that salary negotiation is some kind of a game, such as the haggling done when buying a used car. It is a serious business that has a major impact on your future earnings. However, you must have the correct mental attitude to succeed. Approach salary negotiation with a "win-win" philosophy. At the end of the negotiations, both the employer and job-seeker should be happy with the results.

12. **FALSE.** If the job offered is really your dream job, then there must be some greater intangible benefits that attract you, more than just the salary. If this job is a stepping-stone in your long-term career plan then you should accept a lower salary in the short term for the greater benefits expected in the long term. Remember, if you negotiate well, you may be able to get some other form of compensation, such as a signing-on bonus or a reduced probation period.

13. **FALSE.** Whether the offer is acceptable or not, you will be too tense during interviews to take a well thought out and objective decision. Therefore, your strategy should be to thank the employer and ask for time to consider all aspects of the offer. You should take time to look closely at the offer and decide if and how much more you wish to negotiate on the package.

14. **FALSE.** The proper tone for negotiations is always conversational, not confrontational. You should never make any kind of demand when negotiating. Instead, make requests. If the negotiations seem stalled, it may be a sign that the employer is not going to negotiate any further.

15. **FALSE.** Once you have accepted the offer, your negotiating power is almost gone. If you attempt to negotiate after accepting the offer you will appear untrustworthy, indecisive or simply greedy. Once an employer has made you an offer, your strategy is to thank the employer for the offer, express your interest and enthusiasm in the job and the company, but ask for time to review the details of the offer.

16. **FALSE.** Perhaps this idea is the main reason why many job-seekers do not negotiate job offers. You risk very little, but have much to gain in future compensation, retirement benefits, and various perquisites if you negotiate using the principles set down in this book. Why spend all the time and effort to conduct research on salary and compensation if you do not use it to your benefit? Have confidence in yourself and your research. All you need to negotiate a job offer is to know the rules and etiquette of negotiating. It is not necessary to learn how to be a master negotiator. If you are not comfortable in face-to-face negotiations, make a counter-proposal in writing.

17. **TRUE.** It is important to know when to call a halt to negotiations and either accept or decline the offer. During negotiations, watch out for the signs indicating that the employer is not willing to negotiate any further. They include:

    - The employer has stopped responding to your counter proposals.

- The employer's concessions are becoming minuscule, if at all.
- The employer says: "Enough!"

18. **FALSE.** Remember that interviewing is somewhat like dating. Both the employer and the job-seeker are testing the waters, deciding how much they like each other and whether the chemistry between them is right. To mention a different employer during the negotiations is asking for trouble. You run the risk of losing credibility with all your potential employers as they may check with each other. Keep all negotiations separate although you may generally mention that you are considering other offers without naming names or being specific.

19. **TRUE.** You lose nothing by asking for some other form of compensation if the salary itself is too low and not negotiable any further. At the most, the request may be turned down.

20. **FALSE.** When employers mention a specific deadline, they are quite serious about it. Respond within the timeframe with a counteroffer or accept the offer as is. Otherwise the offer is very likely to be withdrawn. If you are in a job market where employees with your talents are in high demand, the employer may be trying to force your hand before you get other competing offers. It may also be that the position requires to be filled fast e.g., for a project about to start. On the other hand, if you feel that the employer is merely trying to intimidate you and force your hand, then think long and hard before you agree to work for such an employer!

21. **FALSE.** The offer with the highest salary need not always be the best choice. If you are lucky enough to get multiple job offers, do not be guided by salary alone. While salary is important in the short term, other forms of compensation and benefits may have

a much greater long-term impact. Along with salary, also consider bonuses, stock options, pension plans, low-cost insurance plans, relocation packages, flexible working conditions, and other benefits when evaluating the complete compensation package.

TIP

If more than 30% of the answers you gave are not correct, it is a good idea to go back for a second reading. The first quiz deals with the negotiations itself, covered in chapter 4. For the second quiz, note the questions that gave you trouble and consult the chapters concerned. Good luck!

Winning Résumé

—Jayant Neogy

How to write an impressive Curriculum Vitae (CV) that guarantees you an interview call ...And the rest is achievable, undoubtedly.

Your résumé is your first introduction to the employer who has never seen you before. You need to give it the best shot to make the first winning move. The book 'Winning Résumé' fulfils this long-felt need for a contemporary guide on résumé writing that is in line with the expectations of global employers in this Information Technology-driven age. The book breaks away from the traditional world of sequential cataloguing of degrees and job histories. Instead, it provides candidates seeking new jobs or job changes with contemporary techniques to fulfil a difficult task, to produce polished, subtle and refined advertisement-copy about their own selves.

This book is the result of an extensive research, practical experience and deep insight. There are practical guidelines for crafting a winning résumé that will stand out amongst a thousand others. Key points are highlighted throughout the book by using bold text on the left side of paragraphs; useful 'tips' are identified by figures of a wise owl. To point out errors and grave mistakes in résumés 'traps' are identified by figures of skull and crossbones. After going through the book the readers will get a thorough understanding of the changes in philosophy and techniques that have revolutionised presentation of curriculum vitae. It is a sure-shot for success in one's pursuit of an illustrious career.

Size: 5.5"x8.5" • Pages: 136
Price: Rs. 80/- • Postage: Rs. 15/-

Books on Career & Management

88/-

96/-

96/-

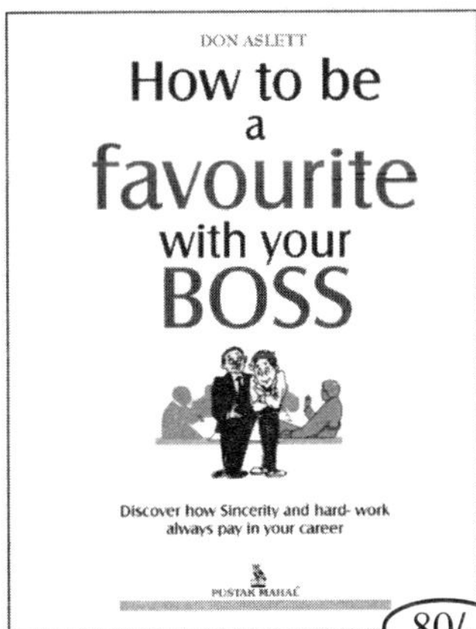

80/-

80/-

88/-

150/-

Postage:
Rs. 15/- each book
every subsequent book
Rs. 5/- extra